Forward by Gar~

When I read the first edition of 'Insights' my
About time 'Roadcraft' the bible of riding, wc
narrative. Something that was short enough i
your attention the whole way through. 'Insights' are not lectures or lessons but the
fundamentals of motorcycling put into a context you can relate to as a biker.

Every chapter of this Part 2 is loaded with simple tips and reminders you can try for
yourself when riding. It also challenges you with things as simple as 'When did you
last practise an emergency stop?' Something that might save your life. Evidence
from many accident scenes I've had to deal with as a professional accident
investigator show that if only the biker had braked harder, sooner, the accident may
not have occurred at all. Yet few of us practise the art of stopping quickly,
concentrating our efforts instead on trying to go quicker.

Rapid Training is not affiliated to the IAM or prepares riders for the Advanced test
yet the principles within these pages are the very basis of what we coach day-in,
day-out. Any rider who applies the things described in the following chapters will
immediately get more out of their riding, probably be safer, and if they opt to take
further training, will be starting higher up the learning curve and get more out of a
day with any instructor.

Enjoy the read and enjoy the ride!

Gary Baldwin
Founder Rapid Training
Accident Investigator Thames Valley Police
Member of the Motorcycle Roadcraft editorial board

RAPID
SINCE 1997

Contents

1. In the beginning

Part 1 of *'Insights'* was an introduction to the skills and techniques used by bikers with advanced training and was intended to cover some of the finer points of riding which may be missed during busy training runs. It also gives any rider tips on how to be safer on the road and for anyone considering it, an insight to what is involved in taking the Advanced Test,

However, when I came to write Part 2 I realised that in Part 1 I had avoided explaining some of the fundamentals any advanced rider must know. At the centre of advanced riding is the 'System of Motorcycle Control' - this describes the order in which things should happen when riding - Information, Position, Speed, Gear, and finally Acceleration (IPSGA). This booklet looks at each of these elements, expanding them in turn by example to show how each of these phases builds towards a complete riding technique. So in a way this could be read as a Part 1 and what is Part 1 could be Part 2.

I've also included some additional chapters to discuss why we bikers do what we do and how we can mange risk better through self-awareness and the application of

Be the best biker you can

good training, by seeing what we can learn from participants in other high-risk sports.

The largest provider of motorcycle coaching in the UK is IAM RoadSmart. Through its local Groups this road safety charity provides coaching in line with best practise developed over many years which helps motorcyclists get more out of their machines whilst instilling skills that make them safer. RoSPA (Royal Society for the Prevention of Accidents) runs similar courses and other commercial providers offer advanced riding tuition from one-day ride-outs to longer courses and tours.

On-the-road training must be delivered by trained instructors, many who have qualified as Police Class 1 riders themselves or in the case of the IAM RoadSmart are certified by Institute of the Motor Industry (IMI). They are known as Observers but carry out the same coaching as commercial Instructors. Usually on-the-road training takes the form of an instructor and one or two candidates with structured pre-ride briefs and de-briefs covering events that will have happened on the ride and to highlight any learning points.

So whilst your mates may have their ideas on how to ride, for the price of a new front tyre you can get professional training from trained coaches to an Advanced level. Then its up to you how you use that knowledge and skill.

'Riding a bike to an advanced level is a skill which once acquired enhances the pleasure you get from doing something complex well, and it could save your life.'

2. Before the Ride

The sun's out, it's warm, the roads dry and you know time's right for that ride. The bike's had it's cover pulled off and been wheeled out of the garage. It's glinting in the sunlight and I guess as long as the tyres look round and the engine starts everything should be okay. All you need to do now is pull on the helmet and gloves, throw a leg over and we're away…. But when did you last do a full pre-ride check of the machine you're about to trust out there in the tarmac jungle?

On test it's not unusual for the examiner to ask you to imagine a scenario where you've been away on holiday and not ridden your bike for a month. 'What checks would you carry out before riding?' will be the question.

There are many pre-ride check-lists you can use to make sure everything is in order. Probably the simplest one to remember is POWDDERSS - or Powders with a double 'd' and a double 's' (no, it's not dyslexic).

Petrol   Easy, have you enough to get to the next garage or your destination?

Oil   Does the engine have any ? Better still, is it at the right level - sight-glass/ dipstick? Is the brake fluid at the correct level?

Around the front check the forks seals for signs of leakage, tyre for tread depth or damage, and run of brake hoses and cables.

Water   Yes, most bike engines require coolant. Only do you know where the header tank is and can you see the level marks and coolant without a torch?

Drive   Those lucky enough to have shaft-drive can skip this one but for the rest of us has the chain been lubricated recently and is it adjusted so it no longer drags on the floor?

Damage   (The Second D) - Is there anything broken, come unscrewed, or held on with sticky tape that needs a proper look at ? Is the seat secure and locked down? Are the brake hoses secure with no signs of fluid leakage?

Electrics   Is your headlight actually working? Do those blinky things actually flash? Does your rear brake light work from both the handlebar and foot levers? Do all the warning lights go off as expected once you start the engine?

Rubber   Those black circles (on the wheels, not round your eyes) are they correctly inflated? When did you last actually check? Are they legal with 1mm of tread over 3/4 of their width all the way round? So no flat spots. Also check for any bulges, tears, embedded flints, stones or nails as punctures are the most common cause of breakdowns for bikes.

Bike tyres are not like car tyres. They are much more sensitive to pressure and need a minimum tread depth to get to the right operating temperature. Yes, just like race tyres, bike tyres need to warm up and they do that by the blocks of tread moving around on the surface. No tread and they won't warm up, plus they won't move any water out of the way making them both cold, hard, and very slippery. (No, they don't become 'slicks' with increased grip in the dry as they wear out).

Steering/Suspension   Do the handlebars move from lock-to-lock freely without trapping cables? Does the suspension go up and down smoothly and are the dampers working? Pogo sticks are not much fun to ride. Are there any funny knocking noises if you rock the bike back and forth with the front brake on when off the stand? Are there any traces of oil around the fork seals?

Self   Are you fit to ride? Have you taken a moment to 'get in the zone'? See 'Insights Part 1' for the full low-down on how to check-out yourself, but you are the most valuable thing on the bike so look after yourself.

Rolling Brake Check   Finally, as you set off remember to do a rolling brake check. Do the front and back brakes both work as expected when applied at low speed? (Just remember to check your mirrors before doing this though if you've reached on the road before checking……..).

POW(DD)ER(SS)

3. Information

There's no excuse for 'Suddenly.........'

Wherever you go, or whatever you look at, your brain's harvesting information. Your smart phone is doing the same, where you are, where you've been, the 'WhatsApp' photo you sent, the phone call you made - that website you visited. It's estimated that the information in an average smartphone would cover around 30,000 A4 pages if it was all printed out.

Fortunately your brain discards most of the information you gather as not being relevant to what you're doing or thinking about at the time. Otherwise you'd probably have run out of brain storage by age 7. However, this behaviour continues when people are driving, with most of the information around us being ignored, or discarded. That's not because we have brains that are lazy, it's just doing what it always does. This though is not good when riding a motorbike and so your brain needs to be trained to act differently when you're out riding.

It's instinctive for your eyes to focus on things that are closest to you. After all in the natural world that's where harm is likely to come from. But that isn't the situation on the road where danger can be developing 200m away and the sooner you see it the better. At first it's really hard to train your eyes to look that far ahead. If you've not been doing this so far try it. How far can you see ahead? How much more time does that give you to react?

How many times do you see other road users simply following the vehicle in front, looking at, and only reacting, when brake lights come on? In this situation they are minimising the mental effort required to undertake a complicated task and are therefore relying on someone they haven't even met to do all the complicated stuff of reading the road, identifying hazards, and taking the correct action to get along safely. You might indeed find yourself doing this on the way home after a long day at work - just how scary is that?

What's this 'information stuff' and how does it affect our riding?

The very first element of the System of Motorcycle Control (IPSGA) is 'I' - for 'Information'

Information has three aspects to it; **T**aking it in; **U**sing it to form a riding plan; then, **G**iving other road users clues as to our intentions. Take-Use-Give or '**TUG**' for short.

The information element of riding is a continuous process as the situation around you changes as you progress. Your riding plan of only 3 seconds ago may be modified by that big truck that's just appeared around the corner ahead, signalling to turn right into the junction just in front of you.

It could as easily be called 'Looking' as that's what we all do when riding so we don't bump into things - but are we really 'seeing'?

So what might I may be missing?

Answer: Probably loads if you've not actually been looking for it, know where to look, or even understand what you're looking at. The UK has probably one of the best signposted road networks in the world with councils spending millions on warning signs giving information away for free, yet most people don't read them. (Just think, how many warning road signs do you actually notice and read?)

Lets take as an example a rural road with a sharp bend coming up ahead. The first thing you will probably see is a red bordered triangular warning sign in the hedge with a curved black arrow on it. Funnily the direction of the arrow shows in which direction the road ahead goes, to the right or to the left.

The triangle sign may have another sign underneath it. Possibly 'Reduce Speed Now' or an advisory speed. Advisory speeds are mounted within a rectangular information box. Both could also be mounted on a yellow background to further highlight the sign.

Next the centreline will become a hazard line. (See the '*Insights Part 1*' on White

Other information may be within the warning sign.
This bend also has two junctions and an advisory speed.

Lines if you're unsure what a hazard line is).

This may be swiftly followed by two large white arrows painted in the middle of the

10

road telling you to return to your side of the road 50m before a solid white line appears. In addition to this a solid white line may also have been painted on the near-side edge of the road to highlight the carriageway. The word 'SLOW" might also be painted across your lane.

The road surface may also change to high friction tarmac which could be a different colour to the normal road surface (possibly red) which may offer more grip - or less if worn or crumbling as some surfaces do, leaving loose grit in the middle of the lane, which is not good for bikes banked over mid-corner.

Finally, the council could have painted lines across the road which get closer together as you approach the bend, heightening the impression of speed. Alternatively noise inducing speed ripples consisting of narrow raised ridges of tarmac may have been fitted, again to warn you of the hazard ahead.

There maybe large black and white arrow boards pointing in the direction of the bend. Watch out for Armco barriers - not something that's particularly biker friendly.

That's nine possible different pieces of information all about a single bend, which is quite a lot. Where all this stuff is present you'd think it was pretty impossible for anyone to miss-judge the corner in question, but sadly they must do as councils only put all this stuff up on bends where people regularly crash.

Probably only some of these will be present at the next bend you ride around. Unfortunately there's no guarantee that a bend with just a simple warning triangle sign will be no sharper than the one with everything plastered all over it, which can catch you out, so there must be other clues, yes?

What else can I use?

As a biker you can gather information from many sources about the road up ahead. Firstly for bends the Limit Point will start to come closer to you, indicting a need to slow down. If you have a good high-resolution Sat Nav you may be able to see direction changes and junctions on the road ahead on its map. Don't though use this as a substitute for looking up.

As a biker you can often see over the hedges at the roadside and see where the road ahead goes. You may see that speeding van coming towards you - or the horse rider - which gives you additional time to plan and react before you reach the bend.

Limit Point

Don't just look at the Limit Point - There's often more to see

At the Limit Point you can see the cyclist as he's rounded the bend, but have you also seen the blue van by looking up and over the hedge?

This is in a national speed limit so the van is moving at speed. Ask yourself, 'Has the van driver seen the cyclist?' Has he seen you? Are you both going to arrive alongside the cyclist at the same time and what is the van driver most likely to do - slow down and give way to you, or drive past the cyclist expecting you to pull over to the left-hand side of your lane? What action could you take now to prevent any conflict?

This is a good example of taking information and then using it to create a plan. If you choose to slow down showing a brake light, even though you may not need to actually use the brakes, is giving information to the driver behind - who may be driving with his eyes focussed only on you and will react only when your brake light comes on.

Telegraph poles used to be a good indicator of where the road was going but these are disappearing with the introduction of new technology - and they have a habit of tracking-off across fields, so be careful if using these as your only clue - or you might possibly follow them.

Can you see houses or a church spire in the distance? If so there will probably also be a speed limit change so be ready to slow down. Does that warning sign for crossroads ahead mean the possibility of a car pulling out? What action should you take right now?

Accident investigators will tell you about the high number of motorists (including bikers) who regularly crash into roundabouts, particularly on dual carriageways. Now you would think there are enough signs about those large fixed objects coming up ahead but how many times have you seen the signs at the entry of a roundabout flattened with tyre tracks and broken plastic scattered over the centre? Was the driver really looking up and taking in all the information available or did the roundabout just 'suddenly' appear?

The most valuable information gathering device you have are your eyes so make sure they are working properly. Look Up and Around. Make use of the view you have to read signs and gather all the other information that's out there - then use it to build your riding plan. Remember there's no excuse for, 'Suddenly ......'

How can I 'Give' information?

Having decided on your next manoeuvre let other road users know about it by giving information. You can use those orange blinky things, move your position on the road, and/or maybe show a brake light and slow down.

Read road signs from top to bottom.
Here there's a blind junction just before the bend

All these help others know your intentions and help reduce conflicts. Some of which may only result in a bit of non-verbal communication but others can be painful.

4. The Art of Positioning

Riding a motorcycle is nothing like driving a car. To begin with bikers can do lots of things car drivers can't, like filtering through to the front of a traffic jam. Try doing that in a car and it could get messy.

As bikers we also tend to put our foot down when stopping, whilst car drivers put their foot down to go faster. And of course we do far more overtakes than car drivers ever do - don't we?

What's more your body makes up around a third of the weight of the vehicle so where you put it makes a difference. In a car the driver is strapped into the seat so pretty much stays still and leaning one's head into the corner makes no difference at all to how the car handles or performs. However, on a bike your body position can make a big difference. Many riders will remember crouching down over the handlebars, chin on tank, to get to the maximum top speed - which could be almost 45mph on a 50cc moped - downhill.

On larger bikes the same principles still apply. You may not need to get your chin on the tank to reach the highest legal speed limits anymore but in a corner where you place your weight will affect the centre of gravity and so how much the bike has to bank-over (lean) to take the corner.

Not sure if this riding position is to an Advanced Standard?

When riding on a wet road, being able to keep the bike more upright by moving your body across the bike would seem to make sense. We're not talking about knee-down 'Rossi-style' riding on the road, but your head alone weighs about 4.5 - 5kg (10lbs). Just moving that so it's now over your hand on the inside of the corner means you've moved the centre of gravity of the combined machine. You'll also have moved the upper part of your body slightly too, all meaning the bike can stay more upright with the fatter and stickier parts of the tyres in contact with the road surface, which is a good thing when grip is compromised.

We're not talking here about leaning forward or ducking down to get your head alongside the screen, just moving sideways slightly by bending an elbow a little more. Try it by small stages when you're next out riding and see how it feels and how more upright the bike can stay.

'Position' is the second element of IPSGA

Positioning for the view is not about being able to see the scenery better but to enable you to have more time to plan. Another difference between a car and a bike is a bike is much narrower than a car so we can position within our lane to maximise the view we have down the road.

Time and space are your friends when riding. It's when these two elements run out that plastic possibly gets broken. Being able to see further gives you information on the space ahead, extending your riding plan, which enables you to go at an appropriate speed. The further you can see, the more time you have to react so the faster you can go, or if necessary the quicker you can get out of the way.

Bends

Much time will probably be taken up talking with your Observer/instructor about positioning for bends. Moving to the right place in your lane to enable you to get the best view around the corner - before you start any braking or gear shifting - and then maintaining the correct line through the bend.

Generally it's to the left-hand side of the lane for right-hand bends and towards the centre line for left-hand bends. Then maintaining a smooth line around the bend holding a constant radius around the curve whilst applying positive throttle.

There should be no 'apexing' the corner as you're not on a race-track and actually it's just as quick to go around the outside of the bend as your speed can be higher and more constant. Apexing right-hand bends just brings your head closer to on-coming traffic. - Nutting a wing mirror, or something harder, can ruin a good helmet so keep away from the apex. On left-handers apexing potentially reduces your view and also means you can't be seen by on-coming vehicles until, 'Suddenly......'

If you're approaching a left-hand bend and having moved towards the centre-line you see a skip lorry tearing along towards you, probably about to apex the corner and would therefore be on your side of the road, MOVE. Move away from the centre line to a position that's as far away as possible from 20 tons of careering metal. You positioned to get the view, so now use it to maintain your Safety Bubble (see page 18). It's no good thinking, 'I've been told to ride around the outside of left-hand corners 2 feet from the centre line and that's what I'm going to do' when your right leg is at imminent risk of being removed by a truck's mudguard.

So the concept of moving around within the lane to position for the view is now established in your mind. However there's a little rule you should be thinking about each time you plan to do this and it's known as 'SSV'.

1. If I move there will I be **Safe**?

2. If I move there will the bike be **Stable**? (Is the road surface clean and sound?)

3. If I move there will it improve my **View** (or safety bubble?)

If the answer to any of those questions is 'no' why go there?

Safety, Stability and View

When approaching this bend a number of issues impact on your positioning.

Going to the extreme left-hand side of the road whilst braking, which would result the best view around the right-hand corner ahead, would mean getting too close to the broken edge of the tarmac - compromising your safety.

There's also gravel/mud down the centre of your lane which would reduce your stability/grip as you brake and turn-in to the corner.

A safer and more stable position would be to stay on the tyre line created by cars, just to left-of-centre of your lane where the surface is sound and clean.

It probably means though that you'll have to go a bit slower.

Very often being seen by other road users helps them plan and avoids conflicts. From drivers and cyclists right down to horse riders and walkers on country roads. It also applies when coming to a stop behind any vehicle. Can the driver see you in his mirrors? Have you left enough space behind the vehicle ahead to enable you to escape to the side should it start to roll backwards, or even worse decide to reverse?

I know of a case of a rider literally climbing up the back of a Ocado delivery van as it reversed over his bike simply because the driver missed the drive of the house he was delivering to and he couldn't see the bike behind in his mirrors. (Other brands of delivery vans are available should you wish to try this for yourself).

Stopping here might seem fine as you can see past the vehicle to check for oncoming traffic and have space to manoeuvre. However the driver can't see you as you can't see his mirrors, so he might start to reverse back towards you.

Stop so you can see the mirrors on the off-side which may mean holding back still further or slightly further towards the centre of the road.

How can my Position give Information?

When rolling up to a 'Tee' junction position your bike to help indicate to other road users the direction of turn you intend to make. (This of course is in addition to the indicators you will have already flashing).

If turning left, position the bike towards the left-hand side of the lane at an angle ready to pull away smoothly when the road is clear. If turning right, take a bit of a swan-neck into the right-hand corner of your lane adjacent to the junction, again positioned at an angle of maybe 45 degrees ready to pull away. Don't just ride along the centre line until it runs out leaving you perpendicular to the road you're joining. If you do this it means you're both trying to turn through a right-angle and accelerate all at the same time. A bike is most stable when upright and accelerating in a straight line so try to optimise your position to get as close to this as you can at junctions when you may want to pull away sharply to smoothly join moving traffic.

On the wide open rural roads we all love to ride it's often the next bend that dominates your choice of position within your lane. Other hazards may be present though, such as side roads and blind entrances to farms, etc. which all require you to move your position.

Crossroads are clearly a major hazard and as well as slowing to give yourself more time, your preferred position is going to be towards the middle of the road to maximise the distance from each side junction, assuming there's no on-coming traffic. The majority of serious accidents happen to motorcyclists travelling on rural roads involving just one other vehicle, usually a car and usually at a junction. So take care at junctions, position for the view and slow down to give the other driver more time to see you.

What is a Safety Bubble?

In towns the priority changes from positioning for bends to positioning to maintain your safety bubble. Good observation will show you where the hazards are and good planning will enable you to decide which poses the highest risk and so where to position your bike to maximise the distance from it, so maintaining your safety bubble.

In some cases you may have two or more hazards of equal risk so you may have to compromise and take a position between them. Slowing down also increases your safety bubble. Remember, positioning is about increasing time and space, as is your control of speed.

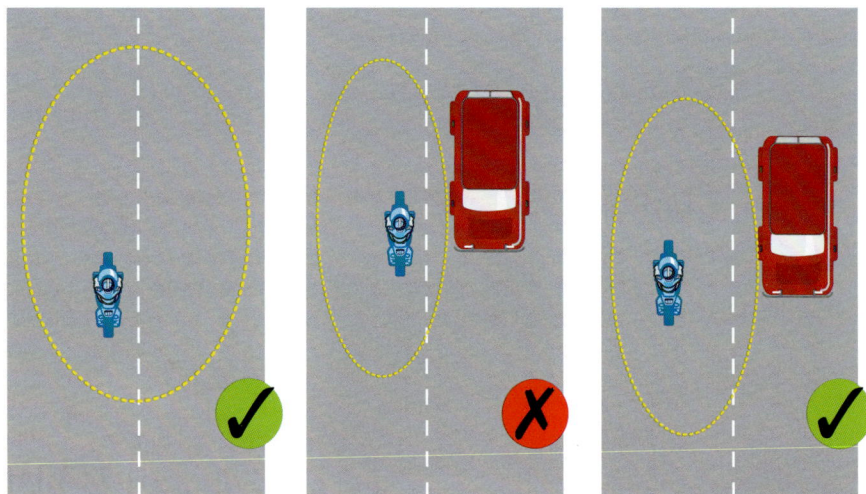

Use your lane width to maintain your Safety Bubble

On a busy high street the greatest hazard could be on-coming traffic so you move to your left to give it more space. On a quieter urban road it could be driveways with high hedges reducing visibility of vehicles that may appear or pedestrians, so you move to a position closer to the centre line to both improve your view and so they can see you sooner.

Bends within urban areas, where the speed limit is 30 or 40mph, tend to mean you can see well ahead without taking extreme positions within your lane to gain the view. You can easily stop within the distance you can see on your side of the road. Moving across your lane because of a bend in town can be confusing for other road users and is unnecessary. Prioritise maintaining your safety bubble in these situations.

Remember in positioning your motorcycle it is for safety, stability and then view. Never sacrifice safety for any other perceived advantage. Always give yourself and others time to react.

5. In Pursuit of Progress

'The faster I go the more progress I'll make.'

Observers and Instructors are always banging on about 'Making Progress' but what does that mean? Isn't it just another way of saying 'go faster'?

Not really.

Making progress is much more complicated than just going faster. Accelerating hard away from the lights just to brake hard for the next set then sit there whilst all the other traffic catches up is not making progress. Indeed you're probably sacrificing smoothness and possibly legality depending on your peak speed. And it doesn't look good to those around you.

Progress is about good observation which enables you to plan well ahead and using that plan to navigate your way through traffic and other hazards smoothly using the opportunities that arise to make progress whilst retaining full control. In addition you will be considering the **SLAP** acronym - Will my manoeuvres be **S**afe, **L**egal, will I get some **A**dvantage, and what will the **P**erception of other road users be? - *'That was smart'* or *'What a plonker'*.

Some good measures of making progress in urban areas are;

* Can you plan your entry into traffic circulating roundabouts smoothly without stopping where possible?
* Are you looking for, and taking, filtering opportunities as they arise?

- Are you observing the traffic flow and planning your speed of approach to red traffic lights so they might change to green as you arrive?

A little fun exercise is to see how few times you actually put your foot down during a journey across town. Challenge a mate to see who puts their foot down the least number of times. Suddenly making progress becomes entering some situations at a slower speed, anticipating when gaps might appear so you don't have to stop. Sometimes it's better to 'Slow to Flow' rather than just rush up to the next blockage to stop. Slow to let situations develop in front of you then plan your way to efficiently flow through them.

On rural roads the challenge is somewhat different. At speed limit changes your rate of acceleration should be brisk and purposeful but not race-like. The same on slowing down into limits. A smooth application of the brakes to reduce speed then a change down to an appropriate gear is preferable to relying on the retardation of the engine alone by closing the throttle some-way off, possibly having to apply throttle to maintain speed before you even get to the new lower limit. Similarly leaving your braking so late that you cross between the limit boards above the applicable speed limit, still showing a brake light, is a give-away that you haven't got full control of your speed at that point.

Doesn't going faster prove I'm a better rider?

On the open road getting up to the national speed limit when safe to do is something expected of Advanced Riders. Bumbling around 10mph below the limit could mean a lack of confidence in the machine or your own abilities. Provided the surface is good and the visibility enables you to stop within the distance you can see to be clear on your side of the road, why wouldn't you go quicker?

Given the agility of a motorbike compared with a car it's more than likely that you'll catch other road users quite regularly. Do you then look for and make overtakes in a positive and timely manner when they are available? (See 'Insights Part 1. for the chapter on Overtaking).

Remember that good observation to anticipate and plan an overtake in advance will enable you to pass far more vehicles than waiting for everything to fall into place and only then start to plan you move. During your overtakes you must not plan to exceed the speed limit and when returning to the near-side of the road don't inconvenience other road users by 'cutting-in' or braking sharply for a speed limit change or corner.

When cornering are you taking a position which maximises your view, using a smooth and progressive technique with positive throttle through the bend? Do you adjust your speed in good time to allow for any gear changes before you tip into the corner? Is your speed matched to how the limit point appears to move? Are you in full control of your line at all times and riding within your own and the machine's capabilities?

On a modern machine it's easy for your speed to creep up as you progressively accelerate out of corners and the fun builds, particularly if riding with a group of mates, so check your speedometer regularly.

The third element of the IPSGA System of Motorcycle control is 'Speed'

What does this mean?

Within the 'System' speed is referred to as being the correct safe speed for you to progress through the hazard, which could be a bend, a turn at a junction, or past another road user. Your planning should enable you to change into the appropriate gear once your speed has been adjusted before the hazard - see the next chapter about using your gears.

The golden rule is at all times is you must be able to stop on your side of the road in the distance you can see to be clear.

How can my slow riding ability help me 'Make Progress'?

It's expected that a rider of advanced abilities can control their bike with a degree of confidence and finesse in all circumstances. This includes being able to ride safely at slow speeds through hazards. This could be vehicles stopped at traffic lights so you can filter to the front of the queue with confidence. (Wandering off-line banging car wing-mirrors, or worse, is not a good way to introduce yourself). Alternatively it could be a slow moving queue of traffic where you're able to keep the under-carriage up rather than continually stopping to put a foot down to stay in control.

The art of slow riding is best practised regularly despite your years of riding experience. It's an art which you will be expected to demonstrate on an advanced test. Can you ride safely at walking pace balancing the controls using the rear brake to control speed without excessive engine revs?

- Can you stop and place a pre-determined foot on the ground or is it a lottery decided at the last moment?
- Can you perform a 'U-turn' in the width of the road without putting a foot down?
- Can you pull smoothly away whilst turning the bike through 90 degrees? This is especially useful when pulling away from junctions or manoeuvring around other vehicles in traffic.

All of these slow riding skills will be called upon at some point if you ride regularly in urban traffic so practising them in your own time and an open space helps keep them fresh. And yes, your slow riding skills mean you can 'make progress' through dense traffic, smoothly and with confidence.

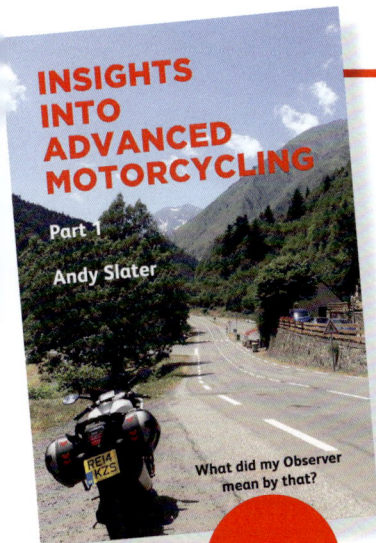

6. The Right Gear

Being in the right gear is an important part of riding. Clearly, how you look is important. Many bikers spend more time choosing their riding gear than they do in fashion shops. "Does my bum look big in this?" is not the only consideration; is it the right colour, right material, waterproof, cool, warm, armoured, and go with my helmet, bike, and riding style.

However that isn't the only gear we're concerned about as Advanced Riders. Most of our bikes come with six gears that we can select from at will. However not all gears will be responsive at the speed you've chosen to travel at. Responsive not only means you can accelerate if required but also will give you controlled engine braking if you close the throttle, for example going down a steep hill.

'Gear' is the fourth element of IPSGA

What does 'being in the right gear at the right time mean'?

To answer this question one has to be a bit 'James May' and understand a little about how different engines work.

Motorbike engines are different to car engines and as most people learn to drive a car before they ride a bike, they naturally think the style of gear selection used in

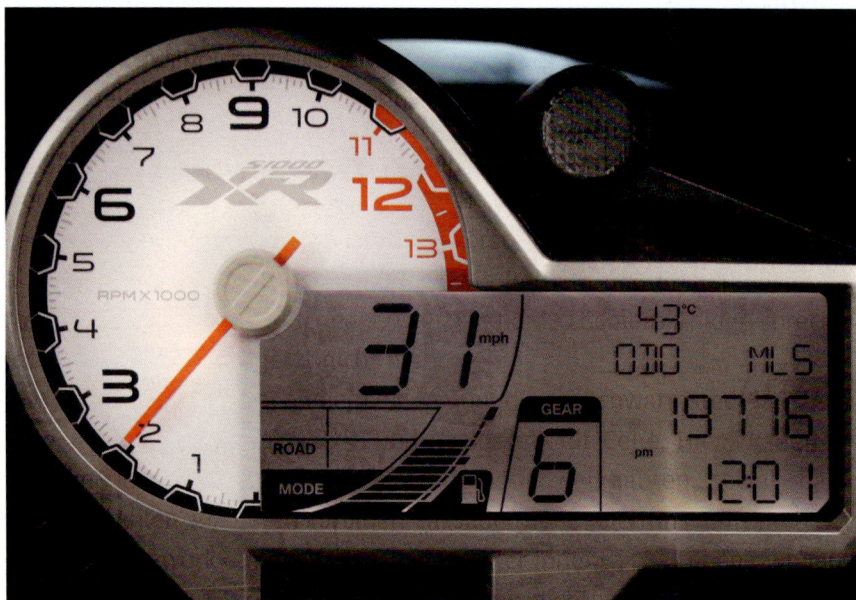

This bike has a four cylinder engine in a straight configuration which means it produces little power below 3,500rpm. Being in top gear at 30mph is just not right.

their car is also right on the bike, selecting top gear as soon as possible. However few car engines have a red-line at 12,000 rpm, being designed to produce maximum 'push' (torque) at low revs to move what is a heavy lump of metal about. Most drivers rarely exceed 3,000rpm before changing gear for fear they are 'thrashing' it. However some motorbike engines idle at 1,200rpm.

Motorcycle engines have to be much smaller physically and lighter, so in a modern bike engine the crankshaft is small in diameter meaning the pistons travel a shorter distance up and down (short stroke). This enables the engine to be more responsive and to spin-over much faster. The result is an engine that produces it's power in a different characteristic to that of a car and it will develop less torque.

There's a wide range of engine configurations in bikes which affects how they respond. A straight four mounted across the frame will red-line at anything up to 14,000 rpm but will have little torque low down and power is maximum at the very top of the rev range. A V-twin though may red-line at only 8,000rpm but produce much more torque (acceleration) at lower revs. Ducati's for example are all V-twins. Boxer engines (eg. a BMW GS) generally produces great torque at low revs which is why their owners like them but with the aid of clever valve systems and electronics now don't feel like the brakes have been applied whenever you close the throttle, as they once did.

It all means there's no such thing as the right revs for all bikes at any given place on the road. It depends on the engine in your bike and the manoeuvre you're about to undertake.

If Mr Kawasaki designed your engine to red-line at 14,000rpm it wasn't just because he could, it was for a reason. So riding all afternoon without going above 3,000rpm is probably not what he expected you to do, nor is it necessarily good for the engine. It might feel okay to you as a car driver but it means as a rider you don't have the response or flexibility available that the engine was designed for, nor can you exercise the control that a good throttle response will give you.

If you find your rev counter barely gets to 1/3rd of maximum revs you're probably riding in too high a gear. Most motorcycles are happiest with the rev counter between 1/3rd and 2/3rds, or at about half revs. This means if you close the throttle you will get some engine braking, aiding your 'acceleration sense' and reducing the need to brake before each corner. If though you open the throttle you have lots of torque and power available to accelerate over a wide speed range before having to change gear, leading to a smoother ride between corners..

Throttle control should be used in corners to help keep the bike on the desired line. You should be maintaining a positive throttle through corners to overcome the 'gearing effect' leaning the bike over has, as it moves onto smaller diameter sections of the tyres. If too little throttle is applied you might find yourself dropping off-line, turning into the corner more acutely than you wanted. A bit like 'over-steer' in a car. Applying more throttle drives the bike outwards from the apex of the corner enabling you to maintain your intended line. As you exit the corner and the bend begins to open out you can start to accelerate - moving into the 'A' part of 'IPSGA'.

Getting the engine closer to the middle of its rev range gives the rider more power and flexibility to control the bike. Here we're going faster but in a lower gear.

For the most part 'Being in the right gear' means you have the engine response and range within the selected gear to accelerate briskly to complete overtake manoeuvres, or to make your turn at that roundabout without having to change gear again whilst banked over. It gives you the ability if the situation changes to be able to adjust your speed without also having to change gear, which may unsettle the bike.

Having completed your manoeuvre and accelerated you may then choose to return to a higher gear to demonstrate 'machine sympathy', particularly on long straights, dual carriageways, or motorways.

7. Now for the Fun

Finally we get to the fun part - acceleration. The hazard is behind us and we can start to wind the speed on again.

The final stage in the 'IPSGA System' is 'Acceleration'

After all the Information, Position, Speed, and Gear selection stages we can begin to crack on again. All of us like the freedom and agility a motorbike gives us and most riders can do the straight parts of roads well. After all a motorcycle is most stable when upright and accelerating smoothly - or as my other half prefers, 'Upright on the centre stand in the garage'.

How quickly should I accelerate?

This clearly depends on the situation. In the Speed Limits chapter of *Insights Part 1* accelerating out of lower speed limits is discussed. 'Acceleration should be brisk rather than fast but be smooth, progressive, and controlled according to conditions'. You should take into account your speed exiting the hazard, the road and traffic conditions ahead and choose a point to accelerate safely and smoothly away ensuring your speed does not cause you to have to brake sharply for the next hazard you may see ahead.

Acceleration changes the balance of the bike, moving the centre of gravity rearwards so increasing grip available to the rear tyre, whilst reducing that on the front. Excessive or sharp acceleration could cause the front wheel to lift meaning

Excessive acceleration will lift the front wheel

27

you have little steering control at this point, or the rear wheel could spin. Bikes are very responsive so sudden changes of throttle input will put unnecessary strains on the gearbox, transmission, and tyres as well as being uncomfortable. It will also increase your fuel consumption.

What is 'Acceleration Sense'?

Acceleration sense is the ability to control the speed of the bike in response to changing road and traffic conditions by use of the throttle so you make less use of the brakes and the ride is smoother. It requires you to be in a responsive gear, to have perfected your observation and planning skills so using your bike's characteristics you can anticipate speed and distance to mange hazards smoothly. As your skills improve your acceleration sense will enable you to ride smoother and longer as the strain of riding also reduces. Remember though that acceleration sense still means you can use the brakes. The manufacturer put them there to be used, but in combination with good acceleration sense the overall ride becomes much calmer, which will be especially appreciated if you have a pillion.

What governs how quickly I can accelerate?

A number of factors may come into play when accelerating. If you're starting to increase speed during the final stages of a bend, having applied positive throttle through to the apex, a balance comes into play between the tyres ability to maintain the stability control you require and also grip required to provide the acceleration you're now calling for.

If one imagines a tyres available grip as being measure of 100 this can be divided between the various functions we ask of it at any one time. When upright and accelerating in a straight line all 100 points of grip on the rear tyre are available for that function. The geometry of the bike designed by the manufacturer means it will go in a straight line unless you apply a steering input so it should all be just fun at this stage. However if you're still banked-over exiting a corner some of that grip is still required for stability, maybe 80 points of it at the apex, so only 20 points are available for acceleration. This balance changes as the bike become more upright towards the exit of the bend, allowing you to use more points of grip to accelerate as less are being used to maintain steering and stability - until all 100 are available to push you forward.

Exceeding the grip of the rear tyre exiting a corner by accelerating too hard can have one of two effects. The tyre will 'spin-up' as it loses traction which can cause the rear of the bike to skid outwards causing the rider to experience what's know as a 'low-side' accident as you slide gracefully into the off-side ditch, hedge, or gravel trap if on a track day.

The alternative is the rear tyre loses traction for a split-second, making the rear of the bike slide outwards, then suddenly grips again causing the bike to pitch upright throwing the rider off upwards, usually over the handlebars. This is known as a 'high-side' and usually results in damage to both the rider and bike as re-entry from 2m at speed onto tarmac hurts and the bike usually cartwheels sideways off into the scenery. There are many YouTube videos available of MotoGP riders demonstrating both techniques.

Modern bike electronics can help control the level of spin, or rear tyre over-speed, allowing the expert rider to retain control and exit the corner still in the saddle despite exceeding the grip of the rear tyre, leaving impressive black lines behind them, but these are extreme tactics normally reserved for the track where the consequences of getting it wrong are possibly much lower than on the public road. Certainly displaying these tactics on test would mean guaranteed failure and if spotted by enforcement agencies could result in points on your licence, or worse.

For the front tyre the same balance of grip vs demands still plays out. As you brake for a corner, or other hazard, the grip is shared between steering input you're asking for and the grip required for the braking you're applying. If the bike is upright the 100 points of grip are available for braking. As soon as the bike banks over into the corner the tyre has to start using some of that grip for steering and stability, so you can no longer brake as hard. Hence the 'System' has the speed reduction phase (braking) before gear selection and finally steering around the hazard or bend. This forces you to get the braking over whilst still upright and before you apply any steering input for a change of direction.

'Trail braking', where the front brake is feathered but still applied during the early stages of a corner means the rider has to be confident in balancing the grip demands of the front tyre. Get it wrong and a visit to the off-side scenery as the front of the bike collapses is your reward. Again many MotoGP riders can be seen on YouTube demonstrating this effect for you, which is much cheaper than going out and trying it for yourself.

8. Is that all there is to IPSGA?

The System of Motorcycle Control' (IPSGA) does has some logic to it. As we've seen in the chapters of this book:

Information is all about looking up and actually 'seeing' what you're looking at and using it to minimise surprises.

Position is an art of balancing hazards, maintaining your safety bubble, and preparing for the manoeuvre you're about to perform.

Speed is not necessarily about going faster but getting it right so you are smoother and applying less inputs to the bike to keep it stable.

Gear means being in the right one that makes the bike flexible so it will respond as you call upon it to track around a corner or as you move into the final stage:

Acceleration - or getting on with the fun.

Well maybe there's a little more to being a successful biker than just IPSGA…..

9. Life would be boring without Bikes (and Risk)

Let's be open and honest with each other here, riding any type of bike is dangerous. But it's fun, exciting, it gives us a sense of freedom, power, and bonds us with mates who have shared the same experience. An experience you can only get if you've ridden a bike, gone to the same places, maybe ridden through rain for an hour for a bag of chips and a coffee. Just to ride back again afterwards!

However, as well as being in the minority, you're also one of the most vulnerable of road users[1]. Even compared with cyclists you are almost three times more likely to die riding a motorcycle than a bicycle and almost just as likely to be seriously injured. It all means regardless of what you ride, having only two wheels when on the road is definitely much more 'risky' than having four. For some though that is the attraction....

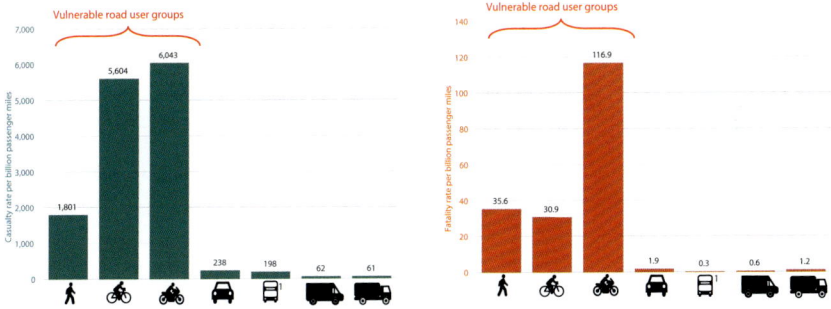

The latest government statistics covering 2017 make for sombre reading if you're a motorcyclist. Not only did casualty rates increase by 7%, but if you're a male, aged between 17 & 24 and live in London and the South East, you are statistically the most vulnerable road user in the country[1] - by a long way.

18,042 motorcyclist casualties of which:

91% were male

30% were aged 17-24

47% occurred in London and the South East

So why do we do it?

In today's society, the avoidance of risk is strongly advocated and there is a desire to 'take control' over one's environment to avoid unexpected outcomes. Why then do we desire to take to the road on a device that surely if invented today, would immediately be banned by those in authority?

Because it's fun - or is there a deeper force within us that drives the need?

Studies of high-risk sports people[2] like sky-divers, surfers, single-handed off-shore sailors, rodeo riders, and boxers have revealed that voluntary risk-taking is often pursued for the sake of facing and conquering fear, displaying courage, seeking excitement, and thrills, to achieve a sense of self-satisfaction in completing a complex task successfully.

When asked, participants in these sports described their approach to risk in spacial terms, often expressing their approach as 'stepping out of ones comfort zone,' 'going outside the box,' or 'familiar territory' to tackle the unknown. Many craved to do something they haven't done before where the challenges were conquering both ones own fear and the elements involved. Some members of the biking community feel biking enables them to step outside the normal rules and boundaries of everyday society.

In research projects extreme sports people describe the feelings they get from success in terms of personal satisfaction and self-esteem. Often success helped them redefine themselves as a person as a result of doing the challenge of their choice. Some compared it with taking an examination where you stand to be assessed and if you succeed there is a sense of self-satisfaction (oh, the Advanced Test????).

Skydivers often expressed their goals in terms of 'self-realisation', 'self-actualisation' and 'self-determination' which through their experiences left them feeling a magnified sense of 'self'. Having done the sport myself for many years I found the challenge of completing complex manoeuvres against real time pressures in an extreme environment very self-satisfying. Interestingly having that aspect to my life made me at the time more risk-adverse in other areas, like driving fast. Why take more risks when you have enough in your life already?

Many high risk sports people describe the buzz of excitement and energy along with a heightened sense of being alive whilst actively involved in what many would regard as risky situations. They experience a degree of heightened emotional intensity and pleasure that takes them out the 'here-and-now' mundane, and everyday nature of life.

Is that why we ride our bikes? Do you recognise any of the sentiments expressed above, is this the buzz you get?

Is it really done without regard to danger?

What many involved with these studies also described though was their meticulous approach to control over risk and danger. This took the form of preparing both their equipment and themselves carefully before setting out. They had confidence in their ability to control many aspects of their situation and through training and preparation they expected to be able to manage the unknown if it arose. The satisfaction they got was from having purposely put themselves outside their comfort zone, and possibly confronted the unknown, they had avoided disaster and exercised control over events which led to a heightened sense of accomplishment.

Studies show that for individuals who knowingly take on high-risk activities their success is due to a high level of self-awareness and capability, rather than an ignorance of the dangers. So training is a vital part of preparing for the challenge. Knowing what to do, practising it, and also being aware of where things can go wrong, is all part of the preparation.

In skydiving the biggest risk is probably your parachute failing to open. You're moving at 120mph vertically when at terminal velocity in free-fall and have just seconds before you'll hit the ground unless you do the right things in the right

Skydivers trust their equipment and training to manage risk

order. But you've practised these manoeuvres regularly on the ground so it becomes almost second-nature. When the real situation arises you can therefore deal with it. You assess the failure, operate the mechanism to separate your harness from the main canopy, deploy the reserve, then assess your height and position relative to the drop zone and pick somewhere safe to land. Only after you've touched-down do you appreciate the importance all that training had on your response and the outcome.

The same is true when on your bike in many traffic situations. Good training means your observation and planning skills are honed and you can spot hazards as they arise in the distance. Taking early actions, sometimes instinctively, means you avoid trouble the vast majority of the time without sudden changes of direction or speed.

Three Phases of braking

When though the totally unexpected happens and the only alternative is to stop quickly you've practised emergency braking many times, so without thought you go through the three phases of braking; firstly braking smoothly to push the centre of gravity forward onto the front tyre, then apply more braking force as the grip increases as the tyre gets squashed into the road, finally feathering the brake as you come to a halt to prevent the fork springs rebounding with force. Only after you've stopped do you consider the possibilities had you not reacted quickly in a controlled manner. Grabbing the front brake would have just locked-up the front wheel spilling you onto the road, possibly creating another statistic for the DoT annual report. Not braking hard enough would have led to a similar result.

So this training stuff matters

It means we can all enjoy the thrill and excitement of riding progressively whilst managing risk - in the knowledge our machines are well maintained and our training gives us the skills to do this well. To embark on the roads without both of these in place can only be put down to innocence or ignorance, neither of which is a good prospect for your long-term health or bike insurance premiums.